Written by Alain Dupas
Illustrated by Donald Grant

*Specialist adviser:
Jack Challoner, Science Museum*

*ISBN 1 85103 172 3
First published 1993 in the United Kingdom
by Moonlight Publishing Ltd,
36 Stratford Road, London W8
Translated by Margaret Malpas*

© 1992 by Editions Gallimard
English text © 1993 by Moonlight Publishing Ltd
Printed in Italy by Editoriale Libraria

POCKET • WORLDS

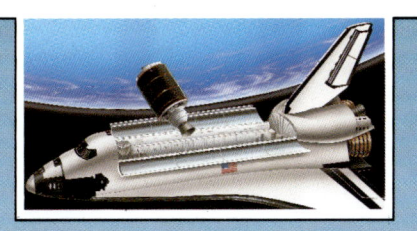

Exploring Space

In our galaxy is our universe,
in our universe – our solar system,
in our solar system – our planet...

THE WORLD WE USE

Robert Goddard fired the first real space rocket in 1926 in the USA.

While you are reading this book, people are travelling through space.

There aren't many yet – perhaps ten or so, out of all the millions of people on Earth, but it's a start. Late in the 20th century, mankind has set off towards the stars.

In the future there will be people living in space stations, on the Moon, on Mars... as well as on Earth.
Who knows? Maybe one day you will take off in a rocket and see the beautiful blue Earth shining in the blackness of space.

The first space traveller was a Russian
dog called Laika, who flew in 1957.

Or, if you don't, your
children or your
grandchildren may.

**Space is not
so very far away.**

Imagine travelling
the distance from London to Brighton
(about 83 kilometres), not along a road
but straight upwards!
You would then be in space, well above
the Earth's atmosphere and there would
be no air for you to breathe. The stars would
shine all day in a black sky. You would be
up there amongst satellites, asteroids,
comets, planets even – a whole new world
to explore.

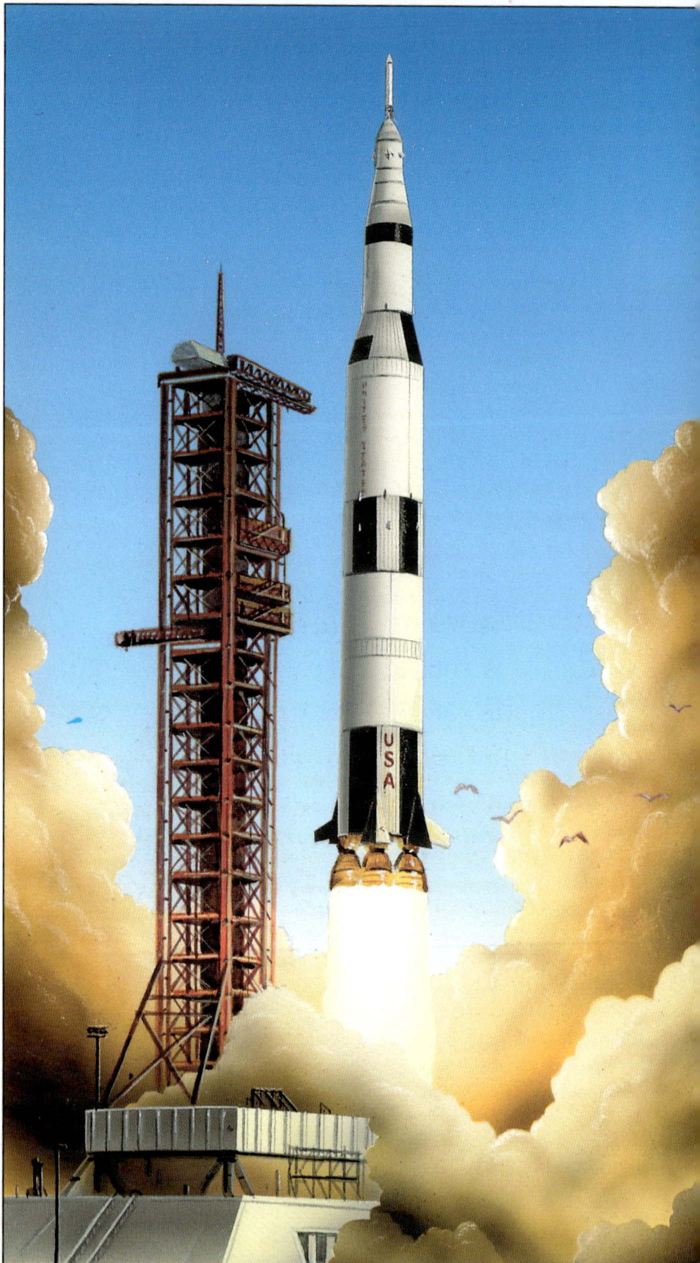
USA

The invention of rockets made space travel possible.

To escape from the pull of gravity and travel in orbit around the Earth, a rocket has to reach the enormous speed of 28,000 kilometres per hour. At that speed it would take less than three minutes to fly from north to south over the British Isles.

Aeroplanes need air, but rockets don't. A rocket carries all the oxygen it needs for its fuel to burn, so it can work just as well in space as in the Earth's atmosphere. A rocket works for only a few minutes, but is propelled at high speed by its engine, which pushes out burnt fuel gases.

Jules Verne dreamed up this space 'bullet' in a science fiction story written a hundred years before the huge Saturn V moon rocket was built.

The first really big rocket

was the V2, developed by the Germans during the Second World War. In 1942 it could reach a speed of 5,000 kilometres per hour, and climb to an altitude of 80 kilometres, while carrying a bomb that weighed one tonne.

After 1945 both the Americans and the Russians built far bigger rockets, which could carry very heavy atomic bombs for thousands of miles, or could be used to launch artificial satellites.

The first artificial satellite was the Russian Sputnik. It was a sphere, 80 cm in diameter, weighing 83.6 kg.

The first satellite, Sputnik, flew into space on 4 October 1957.

It was powered by a Russian Zemiorka rocket.
The first American satellite, Explorer, was launched on 31 January 1958.
The race for space, between the USA and the Soviet Union, was on; the space age had begun.

What is a satellite?

A satellite is something which orbits or travels round a larger body. The Moon is a satellite of the Earth, and the Earth is a satellite of the Sun.
Once an artificial satellite has escaped from the Earth's atmosphere, it can stay in orbit for ever, held there by the Earth's gravitational pull.

1. Sputnik
2. Sputnik 2 and its passenger, Laika
3. Sputnik 3, launched in May 1958
4. Explorer, the first American satellite

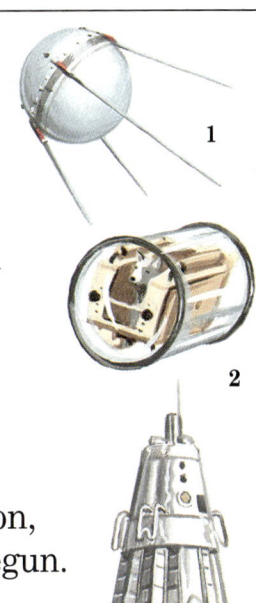

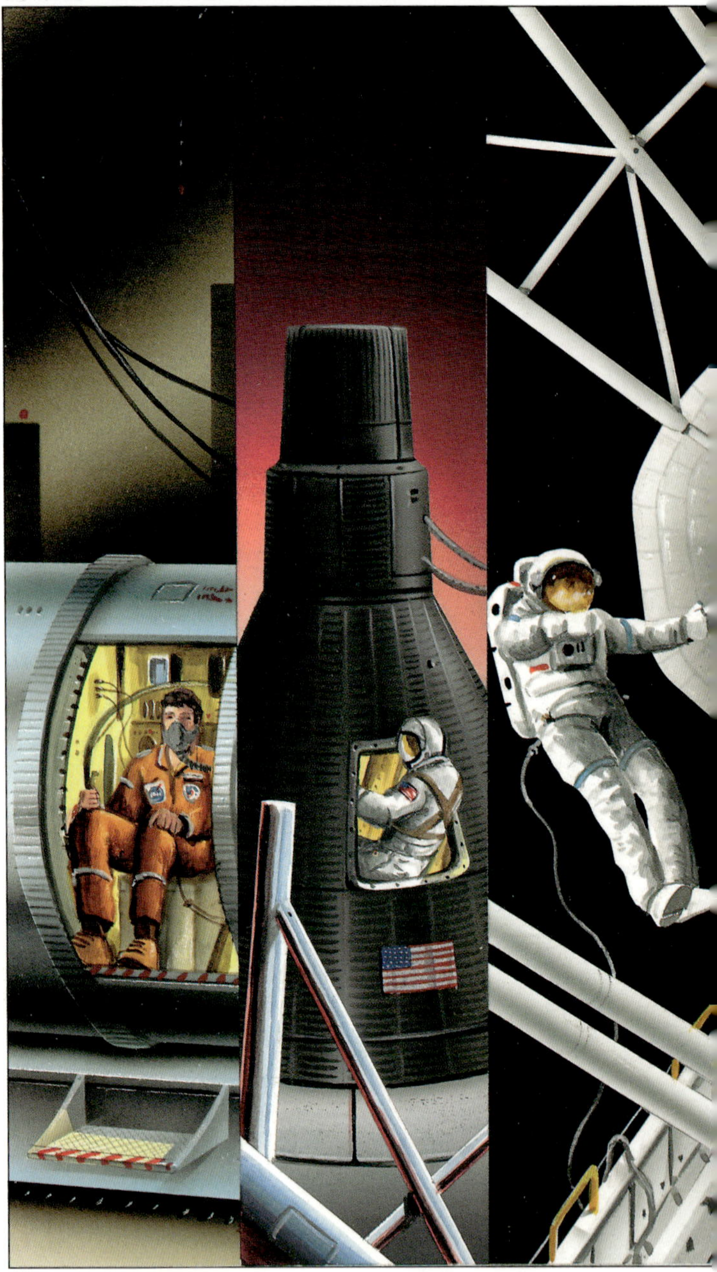

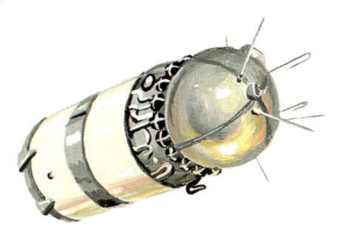

Vostok, Gagarin's spacecraft

A craft which can carry a person into space

must be able to provide its passenger with the air, food, water and warmth that he or she needs. And it must be able to return to Earth once its mission is over, by reducing its speed to re-enter the atmosphere. When the spacecraft is back in the atmosphere the air will act as a brake, slowing it down until the astronaut is able to land by parachute. This is a very dangerous operation: a tiny error could mean that the spacecraft burns up. The Soviet cosmonaut Yuri Gagarin was the first to orbit the Earth, on 12 April 1961. It took him 108 minutes. John Glenn, the first American astronaut, went into orbit in February 1962.

Yuri Gagarin and Valentina Tereshkova: the first man and the first woman to fly in space.

This is what Earth looks like from space.

Men on the Moon

To reach the Moon, a spacecraft has to travel extremely fast: it needs to set off at 40,000 kilometres per hour. And it has a great distance to travel (about 420,000 kilometres). When it reaches the Moon, it must use rocket motors to land gently on the surface (parachutes are no use where there is no atmosphere). And then it has to make the return journey, back to Earth...

On 25 May 1961 the American President, John F. Kennedy, boldly announced that the USA would land a man on the Moon before 1970.

Astronauts travel on the Moon in a small buggy.

The cabin of the Apollo came down to Earth in the Pacific Ocean.

And it happened.
On 21 July 1969, Neil Armstrong and Edwin Aldrin walked on the Moon.
This was the climax of one of the biggest scientific projects ever: the Apollo programme. To achieve it, the Americans built an enormous rocket, Saturn V, and the Apollo Lunar Module, which could land on the surface of the Moon.
In all, twelve Americans went to the Moon between 1969 and 1972.

The Apollo Lunar Module

A space station is the astronauts' home. But it is also a workshop in permanent orbit around the Earth.

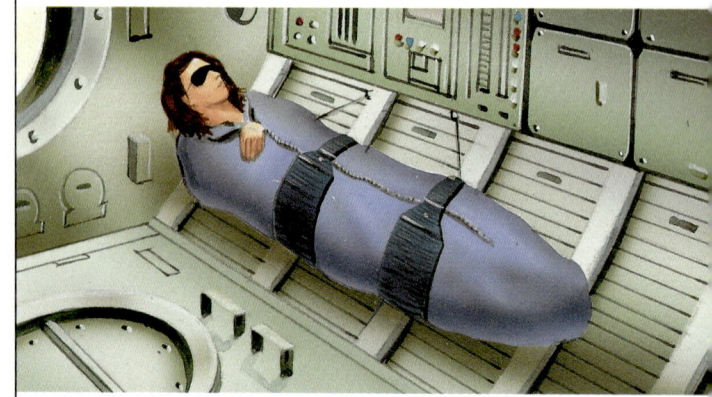

Everything is weightless in space. The sleeping-bags have to be fixed to the walls or they would float around.

Astronauts have to live on ready-cooked meals, which they bring from Earth. Then they just add water and heat the food.

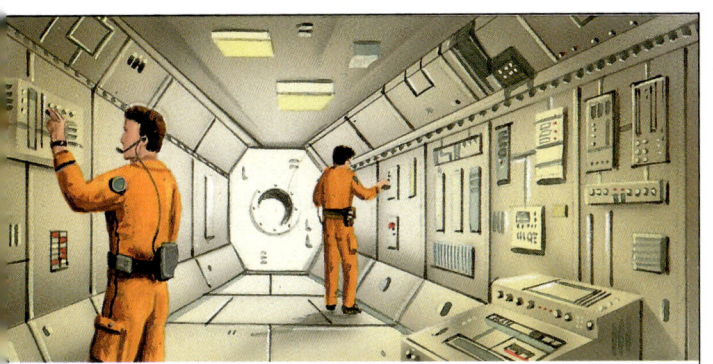

Special cylindrical modules contain laboratories, where chemists, physicists and biologists can do experiments.

When astronauts have to work ouside the space station, they put on space-suits, and travel in rocket-propelled chairs.

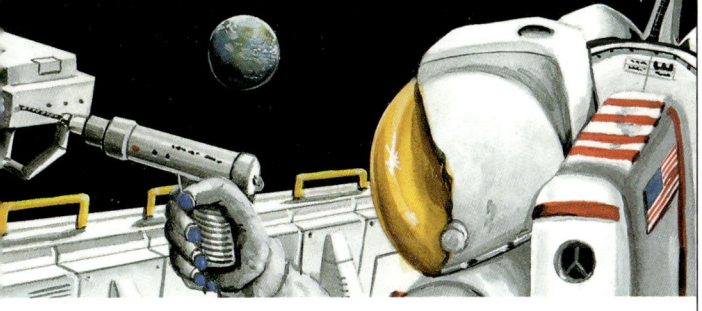

They carry tools to repair satellites and put together space vehicles too large to bring in one piece from Earth.

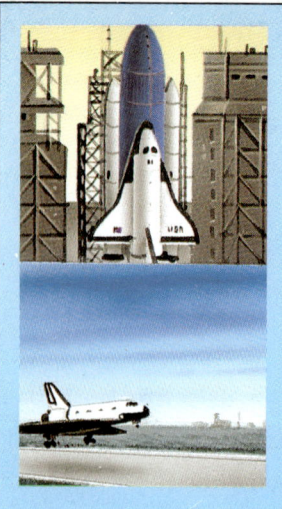

The American space-shuttle taking off (top), and the Russian space-shuttle landing (below)

The first space-aeroplanes

Wings are no use for going into space, but they are very useful for coming back again.

A space-aeroplane can fly through the atmosphere, instead of just falling, and land at an airport instead of splashing down in the sea. This is safer and more pleasant for the crew.

t also means that whole satellites can be
rought back to Earth. And, once it has been
arefully serviced, a space aircraft
an go into space again, unlike a rocket.

he American space-shuttle flew
or the first time in 1981.

 can carry eight astronauts and a load
f 20 tonnes. The Russians have built
 space-shuttle too. It is called Buran,
nd is launched by the huge
nergia rocket.

e American space-shuttle

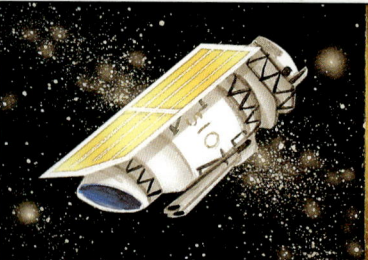

Travelling in space, or going to the Moon, is more than just a great adventure. **It's also very important for science.**

Satellites explore an environment which people knew nothing about before. Around the Earth is a magnetic field which protects us from the Sun's harmful radiation. Satellites are outside this protective layer, so they are also exposed to all the radiation from the stars: gamma-rays, X-rays, ultraviolet rays, visible light and infrared, radio waves, and so on.

These are the kinds of pictures that a satellite sends back to Earth: anything from a single comet to a whole galaxy.

Observatories in space have completely changed astronomy.

Astronomers can now watch stars being born much more clearly, they can see into the centre of a galaxy, and they can observe quasars, which are the furthest away of all the objects in space.
For the first time ever, they can study the whole universe.

The most complicated space observatory satellite, the Hubble telescope, went into orbit in 1990. It has had some technical problems, but it should be able to study stars much fainter than could be studied from telescopes on Earth.

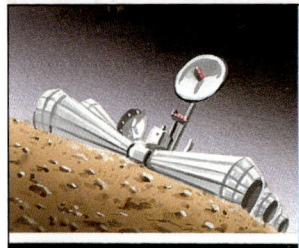

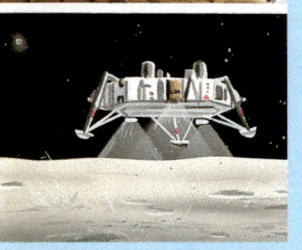

The Viking probes (below) will be followed by vehicles (top) which can travel on the surface of the planets.

Exploring other planets

Since 1962 space probes have travelled to every planet in the Solar System except Pluto. It takes a long time to reach another planet: three months to go to Venus, nine months to Mars, two years to Jupiter.

American Viking probes went to Mars in 1976. Two small robots landed gently on the red planet and looked for signs of life. They found a frozen desert, with huge volcanoes and dried-up river-beds.

Three planets: Mercury, nearest the Sun; Venus, covered in cloud; and Earth.

Probes have also landed on Venus, which is burning hot. The American Voyager 2 flew past all the large planets of the Solar System: Jupiter, Saturn, Uranus and Neptune.

Pluto will be the last to be explored.

Neptune

Uranus

Saturn and its rings

The Cassini-Huygens craft is going to fly round Saturn.

Jupiter and its four moons

Mars is at the bottom of the picture.

Galileo will fly round Jupiter.

Satellites work for us.

If you watch live television pictures of a cricket match being played in Australia, or a concert in America, the signals which reach the television-set in your house will have bounced off at least one geostationary satellite on their way.

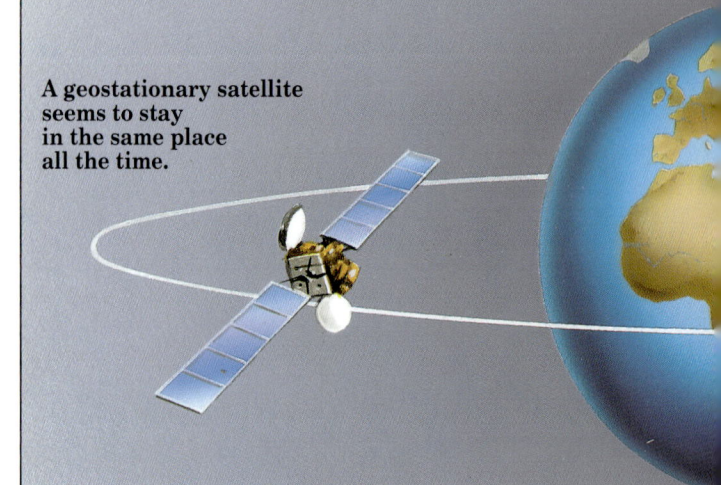

A geostationary satellite seems to stay in the same place all the time.

These satellites are about 36,000 kilometres above the Equator.

Television satellites beam programmes direct to special aerials on houses and blocks of flats. They can also send programmes into cable television networks.

A geostationary satellite takes exactly one day to travel round the Earth. Because the Earth takes exactly a day to turn right round, they look to us as though they are staying still.

At present there are about two hundred satellites in geostationary orbit. Each one of them is able to relay radio waves over half of the Earth's surface.

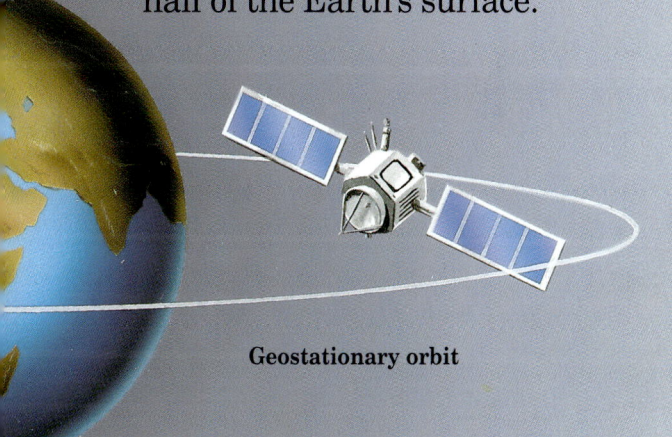

Geostationary orbit

They are used to transmit telephone calls, television pictures, telex messages and electronic mail. The Intelsat satellites are for sending messages all round the world. Within Europe, other satellites, called Eutelsat, are used. How ever did we manage before we had them?

A weather satellite has its cameras permanently turned towards the Earth. It observes how clouds form and where they move.

The view of Earth from space

Geostationary satellites are ideal for studying the surface of the Earth and the clouds above it. The satellite pictures that you see on the television weather forecast have been taken by a special weather satellite.

A satellite that flies closer to the Earth can take even better pictures. From a height of about 1,000 kilometres it is possible to photograph forests and coasts to check on the amount of pollution. And a satellite can photograph remote places which would otherwise take weeks to reach.

A satellite flying even closer to the Earth, say at a height of 200 kilometres, can observe an astonishing amount of detail. From that distance the most sophisticated spy satellites can even detect a person walking around!

Satellite pictures show anything which is polluting the coast, or which is likely to pollute it soon.

Satellite pictures are really maps, in 'false' colours, of the Earth's surface and the vegetation on it.

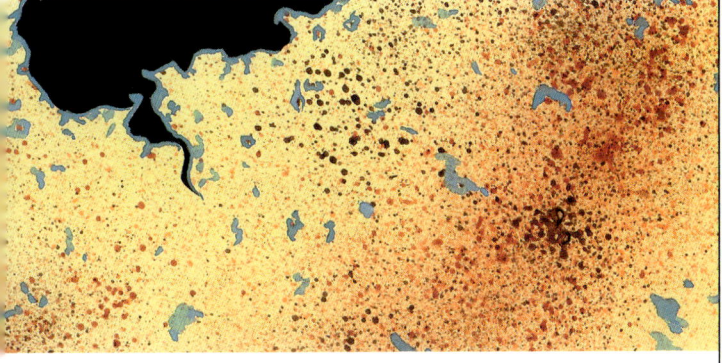

From pictures like these, farmers can work out when crops will be ready for harvesting, and foresters can monitor their trees.

Hermes: carried by an Airbus, and in flight **Ariane**

Ariane and Hermes: Europeans in space

The USA and the Soviet Union brought the world into the space age, and made much of the original equipment for space travel. But in a few years' time people will be able to set off into space in a European spacecraft, Hermes, launched by a European rocket, Ariane 5. And once they are in space they will go to work in a European space station, Columbus. The plan is that Columbus should make its first manned flight in about the year 2000.

Europe joined the space race thirty years ago. The Ariane rocket was first fired in 1979, and the design has been very successful ever since. Half of the commercial space flights today are launched by Ariane rockets. The current model is number 4; number 5 will be even more powerful and should be ready after 1995.

Space stations are getting bigger all the time.

In the 1970s they were small laboratories, the size of a railway carriage.

Today the Russian 'Mir' (which means 'Peace') is more like a whole train, with up to six carriages, which are known as modules. Up to six people can go to live and work there for six months or a year.

Living in space

The Americans are busy building a new space station, called 'Freedom'.
This will be an international scheme, with two American modules, one European (Columbus) and one Japanese. It will gradually expand.

The plan is that in the next century these stations will turn into real space colonies, where hundreds or even thousands of people will live.

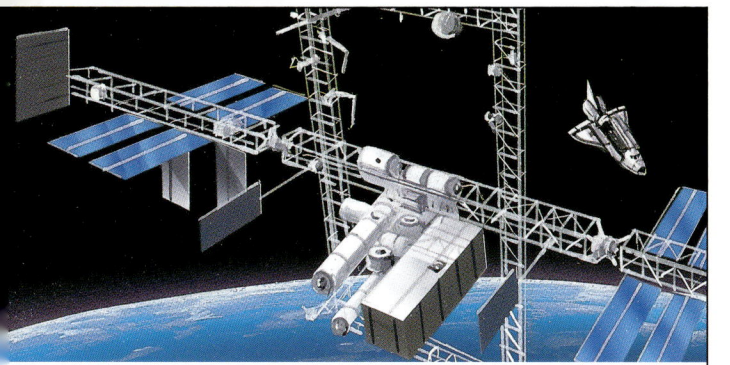

The multinational Freedom space station will be rather like space Lego, made up of hundreds of different bits.

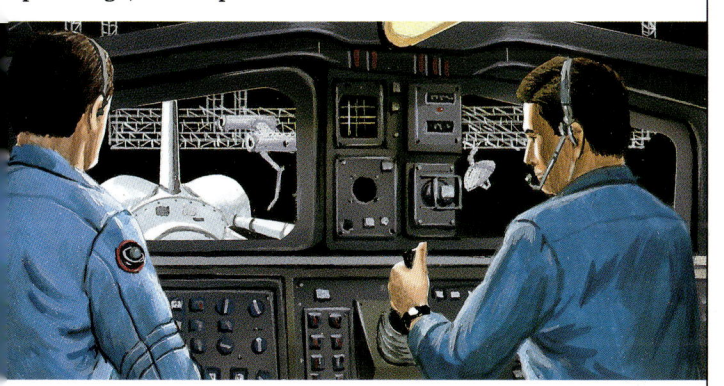

The pilots of the space-shuttle are approaching the Freedom space station.

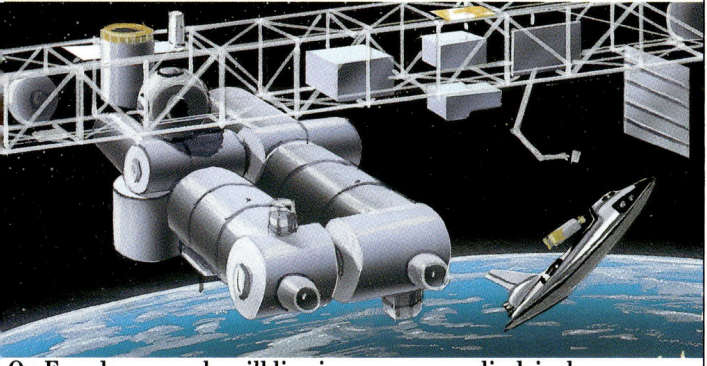

On Freedom, people will live in enormous cylindrical containers, 450 kilometres above the Earth.

Back to the Moon

Conquering the Moon was one of the great events of the 20th century, but visits to the Moon lasted only a short time. Just twelve Americans walked on the Moon between 1969 and 1972.

Maybe in the next century people will land there again. If so, they will want to stay longer and set up permanent bases to use as scientific laboratories.
Substances from the Moon will be part of a space industry programme. The Moon has an unlimited supply of solar energy (power from the Sun), which could power any number of factories in space – and, possibly, on Earth as well.

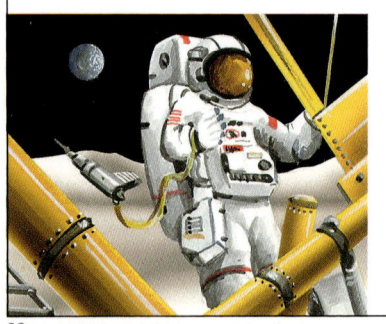

Can you imagine this happening in 2010? Astronauts in space suits are building the first city on the Moon, working by the light of the Earth.

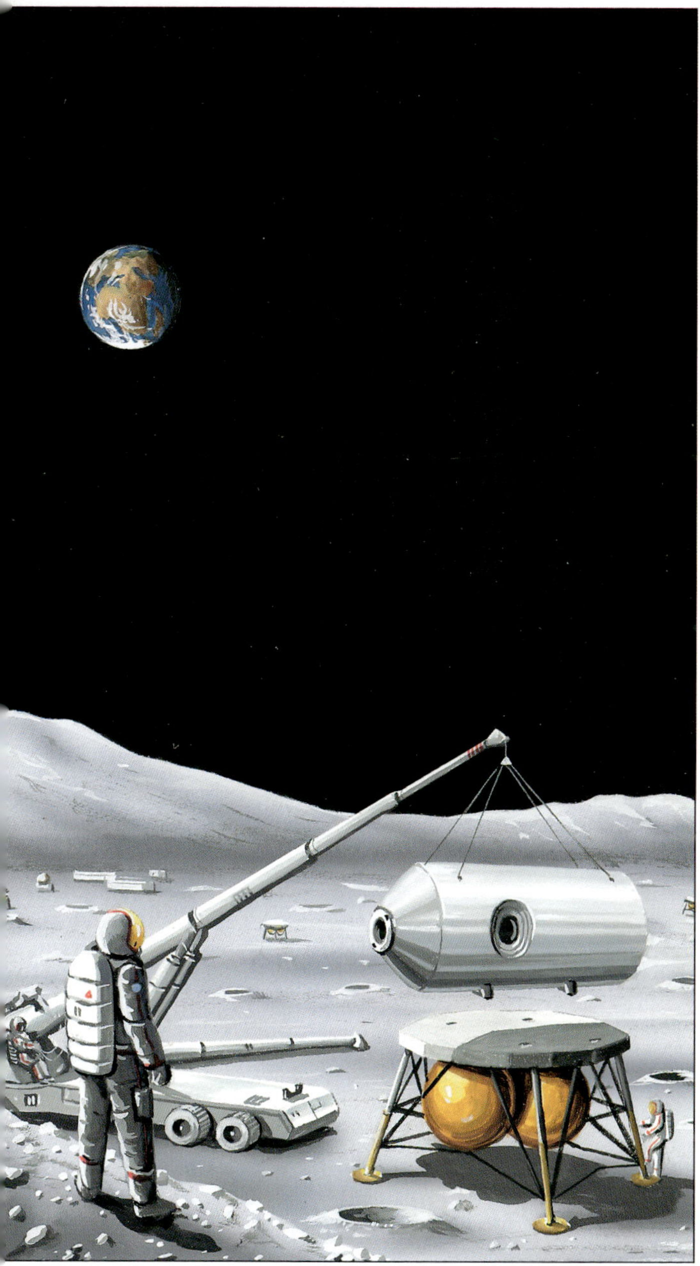

Voyage to Mars

What do you think might happen in the 21st century? After space stations and perhaps space cities have been built around the Earth, people will want to go to Mars.

No-one has yet set foot on Mars, but the Viking probes gathered information about what it was like there. As early as 2005, people might travel to Mars, and by 2020 they could be staying there for short visits.

Maybe some people might stay longer to explore Mars, with its amazing canyons, its volcanoes and its sand-dunes.

The first visitors to Mars will probably stay there for just a few months.

Can you imagine living on Mars?

It would be a fantastic adventure which could lead to even greater things. One day, human beings might colonise the entire Solar System. Perhaps your children, or your grand-children, might be some of the people who do just that.

They set off in a huge space-ship, but they will land on Mars in a small module.

Index

Aldrin, Edwin, 15
Apollo programme, 15
Armstrong, Neil, 15
astronaut, 14-15, 16, 17, 32
astronomy, 21
atmosphere, 7, 13, 18
Columbus, 28, 30
Galileo, 23
geostationary satellite, 24-5, 26
Goddard, Robert, 6
gravity, 9, 11, 16
Hubble space telescope, 21
Jupiter, 22, 23
Kennedy, John F., 14

Mars, 22, 23, 34, 35
Mercury, 22
Mir, 30
Moon, 14-15, 20, 32
Neptune, 23
orbit, 11, 13, 21, 25
Pluto, 22, 23
quasar, 21
radiation, 20
rocket, 6, 9, 10, 14, 19, 29
satellite, 10, 11, 19, 20, 21, 24-6, 27
Saturn, 23
Saturn V, 9, 15

space-aeroplane, 18
space age, 11
space-shuttle, 18, 19
space station, 6, 16, 17, 28, 30, 31, 34
Uranus, 23
Venus, 22, 23
Verne, Jules, 9
Viking probes, 22
Voyager 2, 23
V2 rocket, 10

Are you interested in these subjects?
There are lots more **Pocket Worlds**!

<u>The Natural World</u>
The Air Around Us
The Sunshine Around Us
The Moon and Stars Around Us
Our Blue Planet
Coast and Seashore
Mountains of the World
Volcanoes of the World
Deserts and Jungles
Rocks and Stones
In the Hedgerow
The Life of the Tree
Woodland and Forest
The Pond
Fruits of the Earth

<u>The Animal World</u>
Prehistoric Animals
The Long Life and Gentle Ways
  of the Elephant
Big Bears and Little Bears
Big Cats and Little Cats
Farm Animals Around
  the World
Cows and Their Cousins

All About Pigs
The Horse
Monkeys and Apes
Crocodiles and Alligators
Whales, Dolphins and Seals
Wolf!
Bees, Ants and Termites
Caterpillars, Butterflies
  and Moths
Birds and Their Nests
Wildlife Alert!
Wildlife in Towns
Animals in Winter
Animals on the Move
Animals Underground
Animal Architects
Animal Colours and Patterns
Animals of the Night
Teeth and Fangs

<u>The World of Food</u>
Chocolate, Tea and Coffee
Bread Around the World
The Potato
The Story of a Grain of Rice